TABLE OF CONTENTS

Message from the DHS CIO

Luke J. McCormack
Department of Homeland Security
Chief Information Officer

It is with great pleasure that I share with you the Department of Homeland Security Information Technology Strategic Plan 2015-2018, our first revision of the IT Strategic Plan since 2011, and a critical element toward achieving "IT excellence"– that is, the most advanced, efficient, and effective management of IT and related services and resources, at every level.

DHS' missions are wide-ranging, but our goal is clear: a safer, more secure America, resilient against terrorism and other potential threats. DHS IT has a powerful role to play. New technologies continue to emerge at a rapid pace, security threats grow increasingly sophisticated, and there are fewer resources and dollars government-wide. To adapt, we intend to fundamentally transform how DHS does business.

The DHS IT Strategic Plan is our coordinated effort to integrate people, processes, technology, information, and governance in a way that fully supports the needs of our workforce, our partners, our customers, and the American public, while addressing our ever-evolving mission challenges. It provides direction and guidance on advancing IT capabilities and resources in order to improve the Department's operational efficiency, mission effectiveness, and front-line operations.

This plan was developed through the powerful collaboration made possible by Secretary Jeh C. Johnson's "Unity of Effort" initiative, engaging all levels of OCIO and the CIO Council, whose members represent the IT communities of every DHS Component.

The result: a focused, mission-driven, achievable plan that positions our technology environment to address the critical areas of people and culture, innovative technologies, cybersecurity, and governance and accountability.

The 2015-2018 DHS IT Strategic Plan is a guide for the IT community both within and outside of DHS, as we work together to deliver effective, efficient services and solutions that ultimately provide for the security of the American people.

ENDORSEMENTS

The DHS Chief Information Officer Council

"The DHS CIO Council sets the vision and strategy for the Information Technology function and information resources within the Department of Homeland Security, and leads the delivery of information technology enabled mission capabilities in a timely and effective manner." **DHS CIO COUNCIL CHARTER**

Luke J. McCormack
Department of Homeland Security
Chief Information Officer

Margaret H. Graves
Department of Homeland Security
Deputy Chief Information Officer

Charles Armstrong
U.S. Customs and Border Protection
Chief Information Officer

Stephen Rice
Transportation Security Administration
Chief Information Officer

Robert Dilonardo
Domestic Nuclear Detection Office
Chief Information Officer

Mark A. Schwartz
U.S. Citizen and Immigration Services
Chief Information Officer

Robert J. Duffy
Office of Inspector General
Chief Information Officer

Clark Smith
Intelligence and Analysis
Chief Information Officer

Dave Epperson
National Protection and Programs Directorate
Chief Information Officer

Steven Smith
U.S. Immigration and Customs Enforcement
Chief Information Officer (Acting)

Adrian R. Gardner
Federal Emergency Management Agency
Chief Information Officer

Rick Stevens
Science and Technology
Chief Information Officer

RADM Marshall B. Lytle III
U.S. Coast Guard
Chief Information Officer

Barbara Whitelaw
DHS Office of the Chief Information Officer
Chief of Staff

Sandy H. Peavy
Federal Law Enforcement Training Center
Chief Information Officer

INTRODUCTION

DHS Information Technology Strategic Plan 2015 – 2018

The Department of Homeland Security (DHS) has a vital mission: to secure the nation from the many threats it faces. The DHS vision is to ensure a homeland that is safe, secure, and resilient against terrorism and other hazards. These overarching goals are the basis for the IT mission and IT vision set forth in this document; the strategies and actions of the DHS CIO community are rooted in and aligned with the founding principles and highest priorities of Homeland Security.

The DHS IT Strategic Plan 2015-2018 reflects our rapidly-changing IT environment and evolving mission and business needs, as well as IT's role in every aspect of security and resilience. It outlines DHS' IT priorities and provides strategic direction for the use of IT resources, in order to improve the efficiency of our programs, enhance our mission effectiveness, and ultimately, provide for the security of the American people.

As part of its strategic planning process, DHS cross-Component leadership developed five high-level goals, each with no more than four achievable objectives. In addition, each goal and its objectives were given an outcome; that is, the intended end state once the goal and objectives are complete.

The IT Strategic Plan collectively supports the strategies outlined in the Department's Strategic Plan for fiscal years 2012-2016 and the mission, goals, and objectives outlined in the 2014 Quadrennial Homeland Security Review (QHSR). It is an update to the DHS Information Technology Strategic Plan for fiscal years 2011-2015. The execution of the strategies in this plan is to be carried out under the leadership of the DHS CIO Council.

> *"Just as technology has rapidly changed our daily lives, so too has it transformed DHS' opportunities for achieving its mission."*
>
> **Homeland Security CIO**
> **Luke McCormack**

MISSION, VISION, PRINCIPLES

With more than 240,000 employees stationed around the world, it is DHS' goal to serve as a unified force. In some way, every day, every employee contributes to the safety and resiliency of the nation.

Using the DHS and DHS IT visions and missions as its foundation, the DHS IT Strategic Plan 2015-2018 is designed as a consistent, responsible, and achievable plan that strengthens the Department's ability to accomplish its mission and support employees and partners.

In addition, the plan reflects DHS' IT principles -- those key elements that are the standard for how DHS conducts the business of IT.

DHS Vision

A homeland that is safe, secure, and resilient against terrorism and other hazards, where American interests, aspirations, and way of life can thrive.

5 DHS Core Missions

1. Prevent Terrorism and Enhance Security

2. Secure and Manage Our Borders

3. Enforce and Administer Our Immigration Laws

4. Safeguard and Secure Cyberspace

5. Strengthen National Preparedness and Resilience

DHS IT Mission

Enable the DHS mission through excellence in information technology.

DHS IT Vision

DHS IT enables secure resilient capabilities to achieve interoperability, information sharing, and unity of effort for DHS and its partners.

Who we are,
what we represent,
how we do business:

★ **Principles**

- **People First:** Our workforce is our priority. We create an open, honest, caring workplace where individuals have opportunities to test their potential.

- **Secure:** We are multi-threat and all-hazard ready. We have a smart, effective, efficient, risk-based approach to security. We are prepared and resilient.

- **Innovative:** We provide the information and tools to enable innovative problem solving. We partner with industry to bring smart innovations from the private to the public sector.

- **Integrity:** We do no harm. We are transparent and fair.

- **Results Oriented:** We are flexible, responsive, and service minded. We recognize the urgency of our missions.

- **Efficient:** We are cost effective, efficient, and look for innovative solutions. We share resources.

- **Collaborative:** We choose to partner first, to coordinate and leverage efforts. We are interoperable and integrated.

"Our collective goal is to better understand the broad and complex DHS mission space and empower DHS Components to effectively execute their operations."

Homeland Security Secretary
Jeh C. Johnson

| | | | | |

1 Goal: People & Culture

2 Goal: Innovative Technology

3 Goal: Service Delivery

4 Goal: Cybersecurity

5 Goal: Governance & Accountability

---

1 Goal: People & Culture

Attract & develop an engaged & skillful IT workforce to ensure long-term mission success.

2 Goal: Innovative Technology

Transform the DHS workplace by enabling end user capabilities through access to data & services anywhere, anytime.

3 Goal: Service Delivery

Establish a model for continuous business process improvement that enables transparent, data-driven decisions & rapid delivery of high quality IT capabilities.

4 Goal: Cybersecurity

Empower DHS & its partners to operate secure IT systems & networks, keeping ahead of evolving cyber threats.

5 Goal: Governance & Accountability

Improve the IT environment through the maturation of IT governance & accountability.

Objectives:

Attract, develop & maximize retention, engagement & productivity of a high-caliber professional workforce through inclusive, effective leadership & investment in succession planning & employee development.

Solidify a unified culture mission-focused & results-oriented performance across the DHS IT community increase organizational performance.

Enable the DHS workforce execute its responsibilities more effectively through access to data & technology.

Objectives:

2.1 Optimize the end user experience with data, access, & services, providing cost efficiencies & workforce productivity.

2.2 Develop interoperable technologies that enable detection of & resilience against threats.

2.3 Advance the implementation of the Homeland Security Information Sharing environment.

2.4 Enable end-to-end delivery of mobile solutions that enhance enterprise-wide mobile computing capabilities for successful mission outcomes.

Objectives:

3.1 Enhance IT capabilities of DHS & its partners by ensuring operational excellence, framed by service level agreements that meet the requirements of the mission.

3.2 Create a customer service model to improve delivery of high quality IT services, including transparent expenditures & consumption based costs.

3.3 Advance the adoption of scalable, flexible, cost-effective, accessible services through enterprise & brokered service offerings.

3.4 Promote effective, timely, & informed decision-making through analytic, knowledge-based technologies & workflow process re-engineering.

Objectives:

4.1 Adopt risk-based common policies & best practices that meet & anticipate compliance standards to effectively eliminate vulnerabilities & mitigate cybersecurity threats.

4.2 Enable secure communications to effectively support the mission of DHS & its partners.

4.3 Enhance the DHS security model by moving to a next-generation network security architecture that accommodates public cloud services, improves on current PEP structure, & integrates new technologies.

Objectives:

5.1 Streamline reporting processes to allow for increased focus on workload productivity.

5.2 Improve transparency of IT costs through enhanced service & performance metrics.

5.3 Employ robust governance processes for guiding IT investments that includes roles & responsibilities at both DHS Headquarters & Component levels.

5.4 Promote strategic sourcing or other procurement vehicles capable of enabling mission critical activities for more efficient & cost-effective provision of services.

---

1 engaged IT workforce that possesses relevant skill sets, provides innovative IT solutions & works collaboratively to support mission demands.

2 IT resources, including networks, systems & data, are available for the right people, at the right time, in the right locations, for improved mission execution. The DHS workforce is mobile, interoperable & secure.

3 IT services operate in accordance with service level agreements. IT business processes support the transition from traditional service provider models to new broker models, including transparent, consumption-based billing.

4 IT systems & networks are proactively managed & monitored to ensure weaknesses are identified, compliance with best practices is maintained & risk-based strategies are in place to adjust to rapid changes in the threat landscape.

5 Enterprise IT governance & management practices drive decision-making to achieve efficiencies, maximize investment value & optimize IT support for successful mission outcomes. Roles & responsibilities are clearly defined, ensuring transparency & accountability.

GOAL 1: PEOPLE AND CULTURE

Goal: Attract and develop an engaged and skillful IT workforce to ensure long-term mission success.

The DHS missions are challenging, budgets are limited, and IT is evolving at a rapid pace. Successful execution of all DHS missions demands a well-informed, agile, connected, and unified workforce to anticipate, detect, target, and disrupt threats. Attracting, developing, and retaining the highest-quality workforce that can meet today's and tomorrow's challenges is critical to all of the DHS Components and missions.

Outcomes:

An engaged IT workforce that possesses relevant skill sets, provides innovative IT solutions, and works collaboratively to support mission demands.

"DHS remains committed to building and sustaining a world-class cybersecurity team by hiring and retaining a diverse workforce with experience in information technology, computer science, network and computer engineering, information assurance, and program management."

Homeland Security Deputy Secretary
Alejandro Mayorkas

Objectives

1.1 Attract, develop, and maximize retention, engagement, and productivity of a high-caliber IT professional workforce through inclusive, effective leadership and investment in succession planning and employee development.

DHS is creating a work environment that offers employees greater opportunity for career development and cross-training, and that develops and maintains effective, skilled leadership who foster an inclusive environment where employees feel engaged, productive, and valued. This environment is especially important in attracting and developing an IT workforce with the critical skillsets needed to transform the organization. The Department will continue to implement strategies to close potential skill gaps through vigorous outreach, recruiting, training, and succession planning. Outreach initiatives with universities, industry, technical training centers, and DoD transition centers will continue.

1.2 Solidify a unified culture of mission-focused and results-oriented performance across the DHS IT community to increase organizational performance.

DHS is committed to continuous employee training that includes not only the IT skills required, but that emphasizes development of mission-focused discipline, a security mindset, and innovative problem-solving. DHS will strengthen workforce morale and performance through the promotion of a culture of accountability that recognizes and rewards results.

1.3 Enable the DHS workforce to execute its responsibilities more effectively through access to data and technology.

DHS will empower employees by improving information sharing and communications. By developing an innovative contemporary communication framework and by provisioning flexible mobile tools, DHS will enhance workforce effectiveness in field offices, on the border, and in headquarters, improving service to and the security of the American public.

Example: DHS IT Immersion Program

The DHS IT Immersion Program is a highly interactive program designed to provide new employees with a deep understanding of the complexities and collaboration opportunities that exist across the DHS IT community. Newly-hired information technology employees across the Department spend a day with colleagues and senior leadership, engaged in discussions on Component activities, career management, and the variety of work across the DHS IT community. This opportunity to connect with IT professionals across DHS establishes a strong foundation for a fulfilling career within DHS IT.

GOAL 2: INNOVATIVE TECHNOLOGY

Goal: Transform the DHS workplace by enabling end user capabilities through access to data and services anywhere and anytime.

People are able to interact with the world around them in new ways due to the ubiquity of network connectivity and the proliferation of smart devices. Everyone wants real-time data and analytics. Our goal is to make technologies available to provide the right information, to the right people, at the right time, in order to help DHS workers perform with greater efficiency, productivity, and safety.

Outcomes:

IT resources, including networks, systems, and data, are available for the right people, at the right time, in the right locations, for improved mission execution. The DHS workforce is mobile, interoperable, and secure.

"We must harness new ideas and technology to remake our government..."

President Barack Obama

Objectives

2.1 Optimize the end user experience with data, access, and services, providing cost efficiencies and workforce productivity.

DHS will develop a data road map, including an acquisition strategy and implementation plan, of existing Department data. Building on previous efforts toward data aggregation, DHS will work collaboratively throughout the organization to provide information to leadership and employees on the data contained within the systems, and on opportunities to create accessible data sets and to present better information to decision makers.

2.2 Develop interoperable technologies that enable detection of and resilience against threats.

The Department is furthering the investment in the Joint Wireless Program Office (JWPMO) to improve tactical communications (TacCom), and achieve and maintain interoperable communications capabilities. The JWPMO will focus on a Land-Mobile-Radio (LMR) backbone solution for the Department, as well as a technical refresh for TacCom. This represents a unified effort across the enterprise to assess gaps and obstacles, and develop a roadmap to successful interoperable communications.

2.3 Advance the implementation of the Homeland Security information sharing environment.

The DHS CIO community will continue to grow its information sharing capacity by adopting a collaborative, mission-centric approach; utilizing shared technology platforms; embracing a customer-focused information delivery model; and integrating security and privacy into technology solutions.

This will include evolving an information sharing segment architecture; developing agile and mission-based information sharing platforms and applications; and establishing strong governance, succinct strategy, enforceable policy, and clear standards.

2.4 Enable end-to-end delivery of mobile solutions that enhance enterprise-wide mobile computing capabilities for successful mission outcomes.

DHS is advancing a mobile computing environment to enhance mission effectiveness, improve the end user experience, and enable cost reductions in both hardware and device support. The transformation is already underway and will require strong collaboration with IT stakeholders, customers, partners, and industry to execute. As technology evolves, DHS will move beyond its current capabilities to provide additional features and services to the mobile end user device and application computing environment.

Example: Carwash

The DHS Carwash is a one-stop-shop for mobile application testing and development. The project is sponsored under DHS OCIO for all Federal agencies, and provides a streamlined process by which government development teams can expedite the building, testing, and deployment of applications.

DHS Carwash supports DevOps processes and is capable of supporting commonly-used development methodologies such as Agile or Waterfall. It is a shared service that can be used in the development of secure and compliant applications within and outside of the federal government.

GOAL 3: SERVICE DELIVERY

Goal: Establish a model for continuous business process improvement that enables transparent, data-driven decisions and rapid delivery of high-quality IT capabilities.

DHS is using new IT developments to increase business productivity. How DHS does business directly affects its ability to obtain and implement the latest IT developments in a timely and effective manner. DHS business owners must institutionalize a cross-lines-of-business, cross-Component, and cross-DHS mentality to not only maximize the effectiveness of IT investments, but also to adopt a strong, customer service-oriented model for doing business.

The DHS CIO and Component CIOs will work in partnership with Component and Head-quarters chief executive officers to transform the DHS business model to adapt to the continuously changing IT environment, and to become a true model of customer service.

Outcomes:

IT services operate in accordance with service level agreements. IT business processes support the transition from traditional service provider models to new broker models, including transparent, consumption-based billing.

> *"As we continue to build on our success, we will constantly look for ways to work smarter and become more efficient in carrying out our missions on behalf of the American people."*
>
> **Homeland Security Secretary Jeh C. Johnson**

Objectives

3.1 Enhance IT capabilities of DHS and its partners by ensuring operational excellence, framed by service level agreements that meet the requirements of the mission.

By providing enhanced IT capabilities, the Department will empower employees with unparalleled access to information and services. DHS' philosophy is one of continuous operational improvement throughout the organization by focusing on the needs of the customer, optimizing investments for shared value, and meeting mission requirements. DHS will identify operational strengths and weaknesses, and redesign processes, policies, and standards for the best possible execution of mission requirements. In particular, DHS will focus on removing barriers and avoiding unnecessary limitations to agility, flexibility, and resilience.

3.2 Create a customer service model to improve delivery of high-quality IT services, including transparent expenditures and consumption-based costs.

DHS continues to move away from a legacy, capital-intensive approach and embrace an acquisition strategy that supports rapid deployment, agile development, and shared technologies. DHS is deliberately moving toward a consumption-based business model which involves acquiring services rather than assets, where appropriate and cost-effective, similar to successful practices in private industry. This improves service delivery by allowing customers to pay for individual use and service consumption as an operational expense, as well as add new service offerings during the life of a contract without protracted procurement cycles.

3.3 Advance the adoption of scalable, flexible, cost-effective, accessible services through enterprise and brokered service offerings.

DHS will continue to consolidate legacy contracts and data centers, and increase the use of cloud and commodity services. As a private and public cloud enterprise services provider, we must be mission-enabling and customer-focused, while generating cost savings and improving security.

Our strategy also calls for a shift in the paradigm from builder to broker, from service provider to service consultant. The Department is moving expeditiously into the next generation of Enterprise Computing Services (ECS). The ECS model of acquisition is to establish a portfolio of cost-effective, secure, and reliable computing services that facilitate timely provisioning and delivery of services, and enable mission success. ECS will encompass brick and mortar data centers, IT data center support, cloud service brokers, and ECS facilitators. To meet the goals and objectives of this effort, the strategy includes multiple contracts and a strong engagement with industry.

3.4 Promote effective, timely, and informed decision-making through analytic, knowledge-based technologies and workflow process re-engineering.

The Department will continue to analyze and redesign the workflow within and between enterprises in order to optimize end-to-end processes and to make better informed, unified, and expedient business decisions. DHS will develop and employ technology tools to support and automate the integrated collection of key program information for critical analysis and enhanced decision-making across the enterprise.

Example: Management Cube

The Management Cube is a new information technology tool that radically improves information sharing by integrating the Department's financial, acquisition, human capital, procurement, asset, and security data into a single location. Users can access this data, build models, and develop visualizations to answer Department-wide business questions where previously they could only make informed guesses. This effort is led by a close partnership between the Office of the Chief Information Officer and the Office of the Chief Financial Officer, and supported and resourced from all the management lines of business. DHS leadership can use the improved quality and quantities of data from the tool to inform planning, resource, and operational decisions, as well as monitor organizational performance. The Management Cube can provide unprecedented transparency across the Department's planning, programming, budgeting, and execution processes, including the ways dollars, workforce, assets, and contracts align to missions and goals of the Department.

GOAL 4: CYBERSECURITY

Goal: Empower DHS and its partners to operate secure IT systems and networks, keeping ahead of evolving cyber threats.

The Department's strategy is to develop and implement information security policy to align with the Federal Information Security Management Act of 2002 (FISMA), and to ensure IT investment and portfolio decisions align with the Administration's cybersecurity priority capabilities. DHS IT goals include the adoption of common cybersecurity tools and policies to enable secure communications, along with designing an IT architecture with resiliency as an always-on state, built to survive failure.

Outcomes:

IT systems and networks are proactively managed and monitored to ensure weaknesses are identified, compliance with best practices is maintained, and risk-based strategies are in place to adjust to rapid changes in the threat landscape.

"America's economic prosperity, national security, and our individual liberties depend on our commitment to securing cyberspace and maintaining an open, interoperable, secure, and reliable Internet."

President Barack Obama

Objectives

4.1 Adopt risk-based common policies and best practices that meet and anticipate compliance standards to effectively eliminate vulnerabilities and mitigate cybersecurity threats.

By fully adopting a Continuous Diagnostics and Mitigation (CDM) program, DHS can manage security by comparing what the network looks like to what it should look like, and present the differences in a way that prioritizes the highest risk issues first. The CDM is a dynamic approach to fortifying the cybersecurity of government networks and systems; it provides federal departments and agencies with capabilities and tools that identify cybersecurity risks on an ongoing basis, prioritizes these risks based on potential impacts, and enables cybersecurity personnel to mitigate the most significant problems first. Congress established the CDM program to provide adequate, risk-based, and cost-effective cybersecurity, and more efficiently allocate cybersecurity resources.

In addition, the Department is defining "system health" for mission essential systems and assets, by identifying and evaluating the systems in the end-to-end business processes across the lines of business in a holistic approach.

4.2 Enable secure communications to effectively support the mission of DHS and its partners.

DHS communicates across the enterprise through a vast array of interdependent IT networks, systems, services, and resources. The DHS communications network extends beyond the infrastructure to include mobile devices and wireless networks. Through enterprise mobility architecture currently under development, the Department will advance mobility and mitigate risks associated with securing mobile devices. DHS will evaluate mobile solutions to ensure cost-efficiency, effectiveness, consistency, and security.

4.3 Enhance the DHS security model by moving to a next-generation network security architecture that accommodates public cloud services, improves on current Policy Enforcement Point structure, and integrates new technology.

The resilience, availability, and security features of IT systems must keep pace with mission requirements, and stay well ahead of network threats. Legacy systems and technologies (usernames and passwords) are being replaced with secure advancements such as government-mandated Personal Identity Verification (PIV) cards and strengthening authentication for an impregnable IT infrastructure.

DHS is modernizing its Enterprise Security Operations Center by adopting the Intrusion Defense Chain model. Cyber-attacks often occur in phases—a chain of events referred to as the Intrusion Kill Chain—that are often repeated, reused, and predictable. To more effectively combat a cyber-attack, DHS identifies the weakest link in the Intrusion Kill Chain. This methodology—Intrusion Defense Chain—provides the nation's frontline cybersecurity professionals with a powerful new approach to proactively engage, sustain, and continuously improve active cyber defenses.

Example: Continuous Diagnostics and Mitigation (CDM)

Through CDM, DHS provides stakeholders with the tools to protect their networks and enhance their ability to detect and counteract day-to-day cyber threats. Whether to receive important health or emergency information, or to check on the provision of essential government services, millions of Americans visit government websites every day. While increased connectivity has transformed and improved access to government, it also has increased the importance and complexity of our shared risk. The growing number of cyber-attacks on federal government networks is becoming more sophisticated, aggressive, and dynamic. The CDM program enables government entities to expand their continuous diagnostic capabilities by increasing their network sensor capacity, automating sensor collections, and prioritizing risk alerts. Results are fed into agency-level dashboards that produce customized reports that alert information technology managers to the most critical cyber risks, enabling them to readily identify which network security issues to address first, thus enhancing the overall security posture of agency networks.

GOAL 5: GOVERNANCE and ACCOUNTABILITY

Goal: Improve the IT environment through the maturation of IT governance and accountability.

As a relatively young agency, DHS has made great strides in maturing IT governance. Working with CIOs across the Department's Components, DHS established a robust, tiered governance model that provides active oversight and ensures programs have the key executive stakeholders engaged to guarantee alignment.

Continuing to mature IT governance and accountability across DHS requires every executive, manager, and employee in the Department to focus on creating an environment that rewards collaboration, promotes best practices, and shares accountability so that the Department can fulfill its mission. The Department continues to improve IT program performance by focusing on the maturation of IT governance, accountability at all levels, and leveraging shared best practices across the Enterprise.

Outcomes:

Enterprise IT governance and management practices drive decision-making to achieve efficiencies, maximize investment value, and optimize IT support for successful mission outcomes. Roles and responsibilities are clearly defined, ensuring transparency and accountability.

"Enterprise-wide collaboration is essential to ensure the Department's strength and resiliency."
Homeland Security Deputy CIO
Margaret H. Graves

Objectives

5.1 Streamline reporting processes to allow for increased focus on workload productivity.

DHS is automating data collections, coordinating across lines of business, and making oversight processes leaner and faster. Centers of Excellence for Program Management, Enterprise Architecture, and others will increase productivity by providing technical expertise and resources, such as proven tools for best practices and standards, to program managers across the DHS mission areas.

5.2 Improve transparency of IT costs through improved service and performance metrics.

DHS Headquarters, Components, and the IT community will support each other by forging effective partnerships and providing value-added support services to ensure that investments are optimized and aligned with missions and objectives. The OCIO will work across DHS to promote IT cost transparency that enables customers throughout DHS to understand and control their own consumption-based costs.

5.3 Employ robust governance processes for guiding IT investments that includes roles and responsibilities at both the DHS Headquarters and the Component level.

Through enterprise architecture, DHS Headquarters works with Components to develop a unified framework of roles and responsibilities for collectively managing IT investments. The Department will work across mission areas to establish policies, standards, and processes for IT investments, ensuring secure environments, consistent frameworks, and efficient use of resources.

5.4 Promote strategic sourcing or other procurement vehicles capable of enabling mission critical activities for more efficient and cost-effective provision of services.

In keeping with the Secretary's Unity of Effort initiative, the OCIO communities across the enterprise will identify opportunities for resource sharing, coordination of multi-Component projects and programs, consolidation of activities, implementation of common infrastructure services, and collaborative procurement possibilities. DHS' approach to commodities-related business decisions will be enterprise-focused, selecting current strategic sourcing contract vehicles and enterprise license agreements where possible, and collaborating across the department to develop new strategic sourcing vehicles.

Example: Cellular Wireless Managed Services Blanket Purchase Agreement (CWMS BPA)

The new enterprise-wide Cellular Wireless Managed Services Blanket Purchase Agreement (CWMS BPA) mobile wireless contract was developed through the collaborative efforts of the Offices of the Chief Procurement Officer and the Chief Information Officer. Last year, analysis of benchmarking data showed great disparity in the prices the Department paid for these services. This data was used to identify the need for a strategic sourcing contract vehicle that could leverage the Department's buying power to increase services and reduce cost.

The CWMS BPA provides a comprehensive, commercial, cellular wireless managed services solution that includes managed services, a web portal, cellular wireless equipment and devices, cellular and data service, Mobile Device Management, project management, service desk services, and other optional services. The web portal can be customized for each DHS Component and will allow each Component to access and manage their wireless accounts. These services will provide DHS with streamlined invoicing, billing, payment, ordering, delivery processes, standardized reporting, and a robust means of providing wireless devices and services to its employees.

STRATEGIC ALIGNMENT

Federal and DHS Guidance

These drivers served as foundational elements for the DHS IT Strategy.

HOMELAND SECURITY ACT OF 2002

QUADRENNIAL HOMELAND SECURITY REVIEW (QHSR) 2014

DHS SECRETARY'S UNITY OF EFFORT INITIATIVE
OMB DIRECTIVES | DHS STRATEGIC PLAN | MGMT DIRECTIVES

25 POINT PLAN | NAT'L INFO SHARING & SAFEGUARDING STRATEGY | FISMA
NIST STANDARDS | DIGITAL GOVERNMENT STRATEGY | FDCCI
DHS 4300A 4300B | DHS MD 0007.1 | FIPS STANDARDS
STRATEGIC SOURCING - MD 060-01 | OMB PORTFOLIO STAT
U.S. DIGITAL SERVICES PLAYBOOK | FEDRAMP
WH CROSS AGENCY PRIORITY (CAP) GOALS
DHS SYSTEMS ENGINEERING LIFECYLE (SELC)
NEXTGEN ENTERPRISE COMPUTING

DHS IT
STRATEGIC
PLAN

STRATEGIC PLANNING PROCESS

The DHS IT Strategic Plan provides the Department's IT workforce with a strategy for focused collaboration on achieving our goals and objectives, enabling mission success. The development of the Strategic Plan is an iterative multi-stage process that includes reviews and assessments, aligning strategy to government mandates and mission requirements.

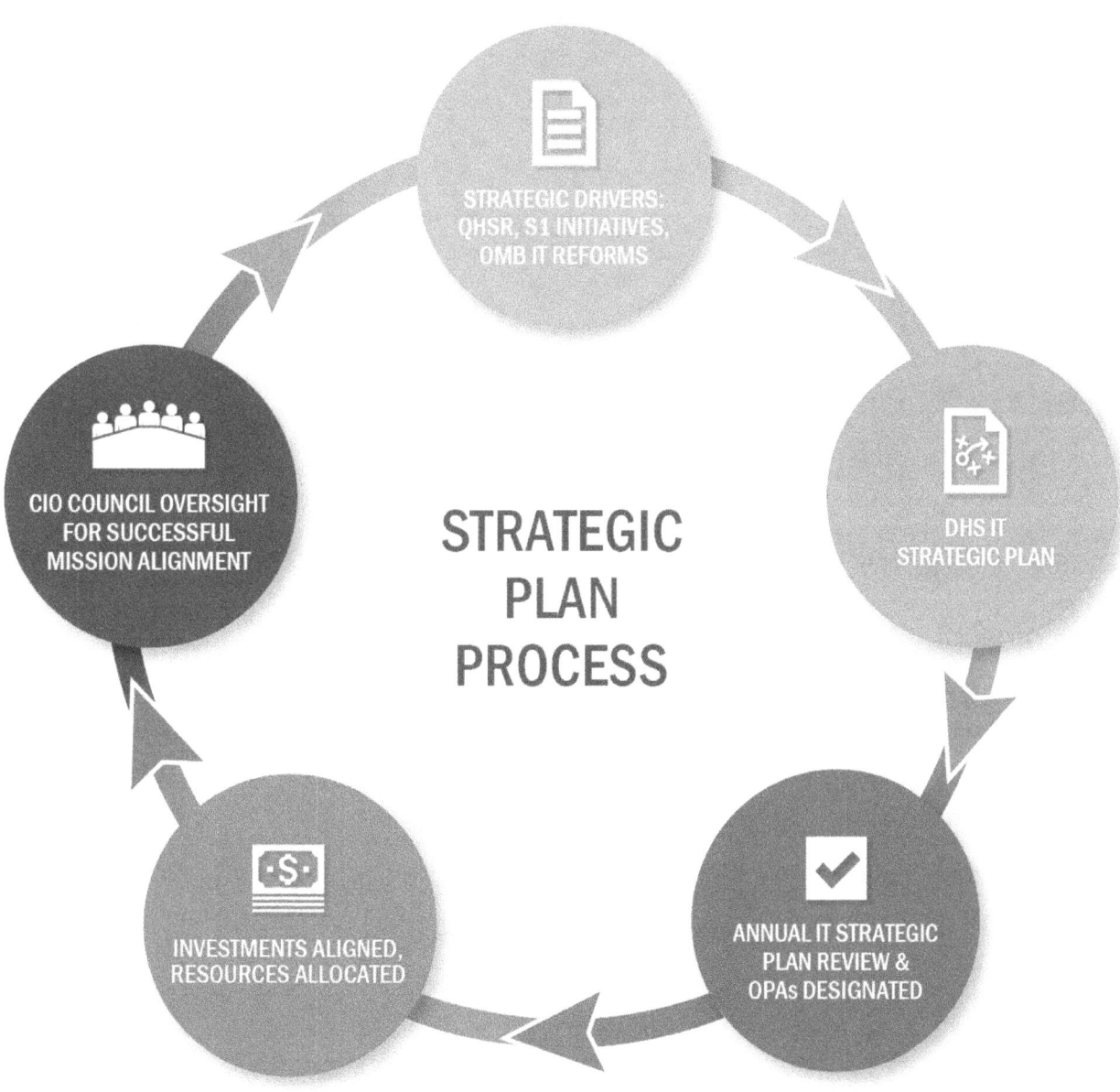

STRATEGIC DRIVERS: QHSR, S1 INITIATIVES, OMB IT REFORMS

CIO COUNCIL OVERSIGHT FOR SUCCESSFUL MISSION ALIGNMENT

STRATEGIC PLAN PROCESS

DHS IT STRATEGIC PLAN

INVESTMENTS ALIGNED, RESOURCES ALLOCATED

ANNUAL IT STRATEGIC PLAN REVIEW & OPAs DESIGNATED

OPERATIONAL PLAN ACTIVITIES

The Operational Plan Activities (OPAs) will guide the execution of the strategy and will be developed annually by the DHS CIO Council. The strategy is executed incrementally through the OPAs to achieve our longer-term IT goals. The DHS CIO Council and the Information Technology Infrastructure Services Governance Board, consisting of Deputy CIOs, regularly review the progress of the OPAs to ensure alignment to the Strategic Plan Goals. The Council and Board prioritize the elements of the Strategic Plan to drive actions and investments toward successful mission delivery.

Tactical Planning Overview

The DHS CIO Council developed the OPAs to support the IT Strategic Plan Goals and Objectives. In keeping with Agile practices, the number of OPAs is small (only six), the timeframe is brief (one year or less), and the repeatable process includes tracking and updating the OPAs to ensure the goals of the IT Strategic Plan are met. Each OPA is led by an executive sponsor(s) who sets the scope, milestones, and metrics to achieve the desired results. OPAs are periodically reviewed and refined to adapt to challenges and ensure success in achieving the objectives and larger strategic priorities.

2015 OPAs:

OPA #1 Workforce: Supports IT Strategic Plan Goal 1 "People and Culture"

OPA #2 Security: Supports IT Strategic Plan Goal 4 "Cybersecurity"

OPA #3 Mobility: Supports IT Strategic Plan Goal 2 "Innovative Technology"

OPA #4 Data Storage: Supports IT Strategic Plan Goal 3 "Service Delivery"

OPA #5 Collaboration: Supports IT Strategic Plan Goal 3 "Service Delivery"

OPA #6 System Health: Supports IT Strategic Plan Goal 5 "Governance and Accountability"